GW01149494

Contents

A Note About the Author	4
A Note About This Story	5
The People in This Story	6
1 Travellers in the Forest	7
2 New Friends	11
3 The Oswego River	17
4 At the Fort	23
5 The Shooting Competition	30
6 A Strange Letter	35
7 On the Lake	38
8 The Storm	44
9 Morning Dew	49
10 In the Blockhouse	54
11 'Do You Love Me?'	62

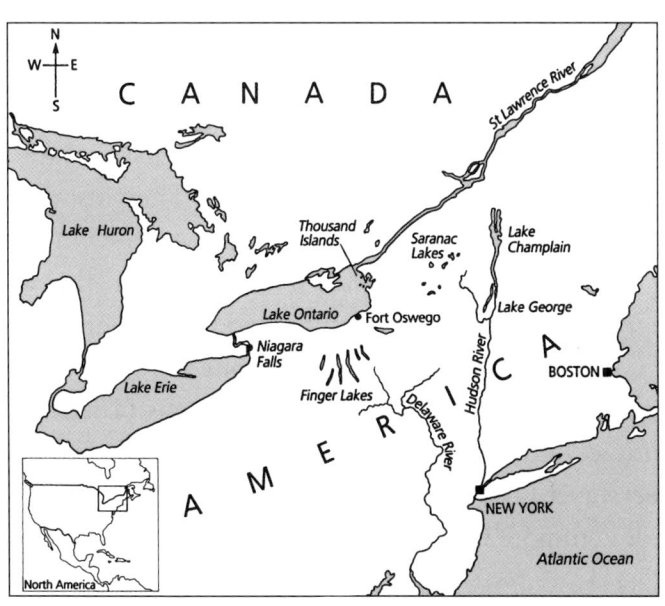

A Note About the Author

James Fenimore Cooper was born in New Jersey, North America, on 15th September 1789. His family lived on a farm in Cooperstown, in New York State. Cooper had five brothers and seven sisters. He was a student at Yale. But he did not behave well and he had to leave the school. In 1805, Cooper became a sailor, and he was in the US Navy until 1810.

In 1811, Cooper's father died and Cooper married Susan De Lancey. They lived on the family's farm. In 1820, Cooper started to write adventure stories. Cooper's stories were about life in the forests and the wild lands of North America. Cooper's most popular stories were about a scout called Hawk-eye. Scouts lived in the wild lands. They knew the paths through the forests and they knew the rivers. They also knew about the birds, the animals and the people who lived in the forests. Many soldiers lived in forts in this wild country and the scouts often helped the soldiers.

Cooper wrote five stories about Hawk-eye: *The Pioneers* (1823), *The Last of the Mohicans* (1826), *The Prairie* (1827), *The Pathfinder* (1840) and *The Deerslayer* (1841).

J. Fenimore Cooper died on 14th September 1851.

A Note About This Story

Time: 1757. **Place:** Lake Ontario, in the east of North America. Today, half of the lake belongs to the USA. The other half belongs to Canada. At the time of this story, there were no independent countries in North America. From 1754 to 1760, armies from England and France were fighting there. Both these countries wanted the land.

The Indian people had lived in this land for thousands of years. They caught fish in the rivers and lakes. They hunted animals and birds in the forests. They ate the meat from these animals and birds. And they made their clothes from the skins of the animals. In the war, some Indians fought for the French and some fought for the English. There were many different Indian tribes, or families. The tribes in this story are: Mohicans (məˈhikəns), Mingos (ˈmɪŋgəʊz) and Tuscaroras (təskəˈrɑːrə).

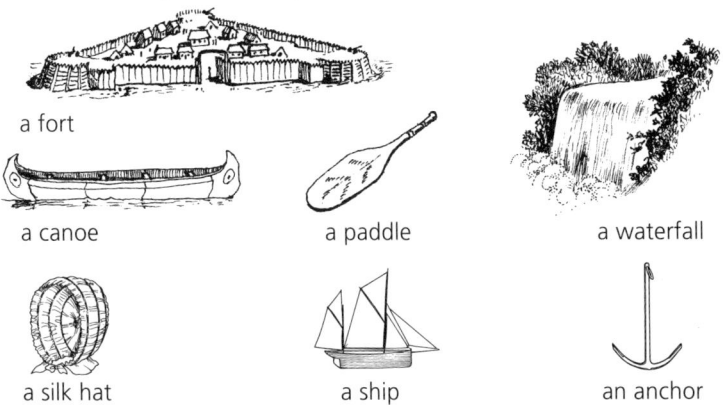

a fort

a canoe

a paddle

a waterfall

a silk hat

a ship

an anchor

Note: St = Saint (e.g. St Lawrence).

The People in This Story

Charlie Cap
tʃɑːrliː 'kæp

Mabel Dunham
meɪbl 'dʌnəm

Arrowhead
'erəʊhɪəd

Morning Dew
mɔːrnɪŋ 'duː

Hawk-eye
hɑːkaɪ

Chingachgook
tʃɪn'gætʃkʊk

Jasper Western
dʒæspə 'westərn

Sergeant Dunham
sɑːrdʒənt 'dʌnəm

Major Lundie
meɪdʒə 'ləndɪ

Lieutenant Muir
luː'tenənt 'mʊə

Corporal McNab
kɔːprəl mək'næb

Mrs McNab
mɪsɪz mək'næb

1
Travellers in the Forest

It was a cold day in September 1757. Four people were walking through a great forest, near Lake Ontario. Two of the travellers were white people – an old man and a young woman. The other two travellers were Tuscarora Indians – a strong, tall man and his young wife.

The white man's name was Charlie Cap. He was about sixty years old. Charlie Cap had been a sailor all his life. He had sailed on all the oceans of the world. The young white woman – Mabel Dunham – was Cap's niece. Charlie Cap's wife was the sister of Mabel's father. The Indian man's name was Arrowhead and his wife's name was Morning Dew.

The four people had been travelling together for a week. They were walking towards the north. They were walking towards Lake Ontario.

Suddenly, Arrowhead spoke quietly to his wife. Then he climbed quickly to the top of a tall tree. After a minute, he climbed down to the ground. He spoke to the white people.

'I see some smoke from a fire,' he said. 'I see it and I smell it. Stay here! Morning Dew will stay with you. I will go forward. There is danger in the forest!'

The Tuscarora walked away through the trees.

Mabel spoke to the Indian's wife.

'Morning Dew, is there danger here?' she asked.

'Arrowhead saw the smoke from a fire,' answered the woman. 'Somebody is near us in the forest. My husband will find them. There are many enemies in the forest – many Mingos. The Mingos are bad Indians. They are not our friends.'

'Don't be afraid, Mabel,' Charlie Cap said to his niece. 'We are near Fort Oswego now. Arrowhead is a clever guide. He will take us to the fort. We will arrive there tomorrow. And your father is waiting for us there.'

'Yes, I want to see my father,' said the young woman. 'I am nineteen years old and I haven't seen my father for fifteen years. Fifteen years ago, my mother died and

Father sent me to New York. But now I am going to live with him again. I am very happy.'

———

Mabel's father – Sergeant Dunham – was a soldier in the English Army. He was a soldier in the 55th Regiment.

Mabel Dunham had been born in America, and her father had been born in America too. Many soldiers in the English Army had been born in America. But most of the soldiers in the 55th Regiment had come from England.

The soldiers of the regiment lived at Fort Oswego, on the south shore of Lake Ontario. The Oswego River joined the lake near the fort.

Lake Ontario was very large. The east end of the lake was nearly two hundred miles from the west end. Many French boats sailed on the great lake. The lake was a dangerous place for the English soldiers.

The land near Lake Ontario was dangerous too. Many French people lived on the north shore. There were many French soldiers in forts near the west end of the lake. And there were many Mingo Indians in the forests near the lake. The Mingos were fighting for the French Army. They had killed many English soldiers and travellers.

Charlie Cap had told Mabel, 'Don't be afraid.' But the old sailor was worried. How far were they from Fort Oswego? Were there enemies near them in the forest? Were he and Mabel Dunham safe?

2
New Friends

After half an hour, Arrowhead returned to the other travellers.

'We are safe,' the Tuscarora said. 'Come with me!'

Charlie Cap, Mabel, Arrowhead and Morning Dew started to walk through the forest again. Soon, they came to a clearing – a flat place with no trees. There were three men in the clearing. They were sitting by a fire and they were cooking some food. Three long guns were near the men.

One of the three men in the clearing was an Indian. He was an old man. The other two were white men. One was about forty years old and the other was about twenty-five.

Arrowhead and Morning Dew stopped at the edge of the clearing. Charlie Cap and his niece walked towards the fire.

The older white man stood up. He looked at the travellers and he smiled.

'Mr Cap and Miss Mabel!' he said. 'We were waiting for you. We have come from Fort Oswego. We are going to take you there. You must travel very carefully now. There are many Mingos in the forest.'

'Who are you?' Charlie Cap asked.

'We are friends of Sergeant Dunham,' the man replied. 'The sergeant is worried about Miss Mabel.'

The man pointed at the Indian by the fire.

'That is my friend, Chingachgook,' he said. 'Chingachgook is a Mohican chief. He is a good man and he is a very clever scout. We are both scouts. We work for the English Army. We work for the 55th Regiment.'

'The young man is Jasper Western,' the white scout said. 'He is a sailor, but he works for the English Army too. He is the captain of the regiment's ship.'

'And what is *your* name?' Cap asked the scout.

'I have many names,' the man replied. 'My Indian friends call me Hawk-eye. My Indian enemies call me The Long Gun. But the soldiers at the fort call me the

Pathfinder.'

'Thank you for meeting us, Pathfinder,' said Charlie Cap. 'But why was Sergeant Dunham worried? Arrowhead is a good guide. He knows this forest well. We were safe with Arrowhead and Morning Dew.'

'No! You were *not* safe!' the scout replied.

'I have heard many stories about Arrowhead,' the Pathfinder said. 'He is a Tuscarora. But he killed a Tuscarora chief and now his people hate him. He lives with the Mingos now. Arrowhead will take you to the Mingos, or he will bring them here. The Mingos will kill you, Mr Cap. Then they will take Mabel to their village. She will become the wife of a chief. Do not trust Arrowhead!'

'Pathfinder,' said Cap. 'You say, "Do not trust Arrowhead!" But we were safe with Arrowhead. Your friend, Chingachgook, is an Indian too! Why do you trust him?'

'You know nothing about Indians,' the Pathfinder replied angrily. 'I have known Chingachgook all my life. I was born near this place. My mother died and I lived with my father in this forest. Then my father died. I was twelve years old. Chingachgook became my father, and Chingachgook's son, Uncas, became my brother. Chingachgook taught me about the forest. He taught me about animals and he taught me about the Indian people.'

'Uncas died three months ago,' said the Pathfinder. 'A Huron chief killed him. Uncas was trying to help a white woman. The Huron chief had taken her. Now Uncas is dead and I am Chingachgook's only son. I trust Chingachgook more than any man!'

'We will come with you, Pathfinder,' said Charlie Cap. 'But Arrowhead and Morning Dew will come too. You are wrong about Arrowhead!'

That evening, the seven travellers were tired. They had walked all afternoon. The Pathfinder and Chingachgook cooked some food.

Jasper Western was talking to Mabel and her uncle.

'We are near the Oswego River now,' said Jasper. 'Tomorrow we will travel in canoes. We will arrive at the fort in the afternoon.'

'No!' said Cap. 'We will not travel in your canoes! Canoes are not safe!'

'I have travelled in canoes many times, sir,' said Jasper. 'And I am a good sailor. Do not worry.'

'You are not a sailor, young man!' said Cap. 'A sailor sails ships on the oceans. He doesn't sail on lakes! Have you ever seen an ocean?'

'No, sir,' replied Jasper. 'But I sail the regiment's ship on Lake Ontario every day. Lake Ontario is a very large lake, but I know every part of it. And I know all the rivers in this land. My ship is always safe, sir.'

'We will not travel in a canoe!' Cap shouted. 'Mabel will not be safe. We will walk to Fort Oswego!'

Then the Pathfinder spoke.

'No, Mr Cap,' he said. 'You will not walk to the fort. You must trust Jasper and you must trust me. The forest is dangerous. There are Mingos everywhere. We must move quickly tomorrow. And we must travel on the river.'

Mabel was listening to the three men. She looked carefully at Jasper.

'He is brave and handsome!' she thought. 'He is a fine young man!' Mabel was in love with Jasper!

'Are you afraid, Uncle?' she said to Charlie Cap.

'No! I am not afraid,' said Cap. 'But this young man is not a sailor!'

Jasper looked at Mabel. He looked at her beautiful blue eyes. 'She is brave and she is very beautiful,' he thought. Jasper was in love with Mabel!

The Pathfinder looked at Mabel. Sergeant Dunham had talked to him about this lovely young woman. The scout remembered Sergeant Dunham's words.

'You must get married soon, Pathfinder,' the sergeant had said. 'You will not be a scout all your life! I will write to my daughter, Mabel. She will come to Fort Oswego and she will live with me. Then you will marry her. That is a good plan. I will have some grandchildren!'

The Pathfinder looked again at Mabel. She was beautiful, but she was very young. 'And I am growing old,' he said to himself sadly.

'We must eat now,' the scout said to the others. 'Then we must sleep. We will start travelling early tomorrow.'

3
The Oswego River

Early the next morning, the Pathfinder woke Mabel Dunham and Charlie Cap.

'We must move quickly!' the scout said. 'Arrowhead and Morning Dew have gone! We are not safe here. Your Indian friends will bring the Mingos soon. I will wake Jasper. Yesterday, we hid two canoes in the trees near the river. We must get them now. We will travel on the river today.'

'Where is *your* Indian friend, Pathfinder?' Cap asked.

'Chingachgook is scouting in the forest,' the Pathfinder replied. 'He is looking for the Mingos. He will meet us at the river. Now we must go quickly.'

'The Pathfinder is right, Uncle,' said Mabel. 'Morning Dew is a kind woman and she likes me. But she loves Arrowhead. And I do not trust Arrowhead. I do not trust him and I do not like him!'

An hour later, the four travellers met Chingachgook by the river.

'The Mingos are a mile away,' said the Mohican. 'We must move quietly.'

The men quickly found the two canoes. They pushed them into the water. There was a paddle in each canoe. The Pathfinder got into one of the canoes.

He put his gun across his legs and he picked up the wooden paddle. Chingachgook got into the canoe and he sat behind his friend.

Jasper got into the other canoe. Mabel and Charlie Cap sat behind Jasper. The young man spoke to Cap.

'Take my gun, sir,' he said. 'The Mingos will attack us soon. Then you must shoot at them!'

The Pathfinder and Jasper carefully moved the canoes to the middle of the river. Then they paddled fast. The water was moving quickly and Jasper and the Pathfinder were strong. The canoes travelled many miles before midday. But all the morning, men were running in the forest. Men were following the canoes.

At midday, the Mingos attacked. Ten of the Indians ran out of the forest. They were holding guns and they were carrying long canoes.

The Mingos ran to the bank of the river and they quickly pushed their canoes into the water. They got into the canoes and they started to paddle. They were trying to catch the travellers.

Suddenly, the Pathfinder stopped paddling. He picked up his gun. Then he and Chingachgook started shooting. A moment later, Jasper stopped the other canoe and he put down his paddle. He took his gun from Charlie Cap and he started shooting too.

One of the Mingos fell dead in his canoe. Then another fell, and another. Soon, the Mingos turned their canoes and they paddled back to the river bank.

Chingachgook laughed.

'You shoot well today, Hawk-eye, my friend,' he said.

Mabel Dunham was frightened, but she smiled at Jasper.

'Thank you, Jasper,' she said. 'We are safe now. You shoot very well.'

'Yes,' said Jasper. 'I shoot well, and Chingachgook shoots well. But the Pathfinder shoots better than anybody. He is the best marksman at Fort Oswego!'

Then the young man picked up the paddle again.

'We must go on quickly,' he said. 'More Mingos will come. They will attack us again.'

———

The afternoon passed. The travellers paddled round a bend in the river. Suddenly, they heard a deep noise. The canoes moved faster over the water. The noise became louder and louder. There was a waterfall in front of them. The water of the river was falling down into a pool below.

The Pathfinder and Jasper paddled the canoes to the river bank.

'It will be dark soon,' said the Pathfinder. 'And soon, we will be safe. We must carry our canoes past the waterfall.'

But at that moment, the Mingos attacked again. About twenty Indians ran out of the forest. They shouted and they fired their guns.

Quickly, the Pathfinder and Jasper paddled the canoes back to the middle of the river.

'We cannot carry the canoes past the waterfall, Jasper!' the Pathfinder shouted. 'The Mingos will kill us. We must go *over* this fall in the canoes!'

'No!' shouted Cap. 'We will all die. The water and the rocks will break the canoes! I am a sailor. I know about water and I know about boats!'

'Jasper is a sailor too, Mr Cap,' the Pathfinder shouted. 'He knows about this river. You must trust him!'

The two canoes moved quickly towards the waterfall. Chingachgook was shooting at the Mingos on the river bank. Then the Pathfinder's canoe went over the fall. It fell down towards the pool. A few seconds later, Jasper's canoe followed it.

At the bottom of the fall, the Pathfinder's canoe turned over. The Pathfinder and Chingachgook swam through the water with their guns. Soon the two scouts climbed onto the bank. They were wet, but they were not injured.

Jasper was a excellent sailor. His canoe did not turn over. He paddled it to the bank. Then he helped Mabel and her uncle. They got out of the canoe and they stood on the bank beside the Pathfinder and his Mohican friend.

Suddenly, the travellers heard voices – English voices!

'The soldiers from the fort are here,' said Jasper. 'We are safe now!'

'Father!' Mabel shouted.

Soon, Sergeant Dunham was holding his daughter in his arms.

4
At the Fort

Mabel Dunham had been at Fort Oswego for two weeks. She was living with her father in Sergeant Dunham's little house, inside the fort.

There were not many women at Fort Oswego. A few soldier's wives lived there, but these women were older than Mabel. There were no other young women at the fort.

Soon, Mabel had many admirers. She was pretty and kind. All the soldiers liked her and admired her. But Mabel had three special admirers – the Pathfinder, Jasper Western and an English officer. The officer's name was Lieutenant Muir.

Jasper Western loved Mabel and she loved him. But Jasper was shy. He did not speak to Mabel about love. And Mabel was shy. She did not speak to Jasper about love.

The Pathfinder was shy too. He did not speak to Mabel about love. But he watched Mabel walking inside the fort. Nearly every day, the Pathfinder stayed at the fort. He did not go out into the forest. He did not look for French soldiers or for Mingos. Chingachgook was worried about his friend.

'What is wrong, Hawk-eye?' the old Mohican asked one day. 'Why are we staying in the fort? There are enemies in the forest. We must scout the paths. We must scout the shores of the lake. We must tell the English officers about the Mingos and their French friends. That is our work!'

'We will go into the forest tomorrow, Chingachgook,' the Pathfinder said. 'And next week, we will go to the blockhouse at the Thousand Islands.'

The Thousand Islands was a place at the east end of Lake Ontario. There were many small islands at that end of the lake. The St Lawrence River joined the lake at the Thousand Islands. English soldiers could hide in the trees on the islands. They could watch the French ships coming from the St Lawrence River. But the French soldiers and sailors could not see the English soldiers. On one of the islands, the soldiers of the 55th Regiment had built a strong building – a blockhouse.

'There are twelve English soldiers at the blockhouse,' the Pathfinder said. 'They are watching the French ships. Those soldiers have been on the island for a month. Next week, Jasper will take the ship to the Thousand Islands. Sergeant Dunham and twelve more soldiers will go with him. Then Jasper will bring the other men back to Fort Oswego.'

'We will travel to the blockhouse with the Sergeant and his men, Chingachgook,' said the Pathfinder. 'And Mabel and her uncle will go with us.'

'That is good news, Hawk-eye,' said Chingachgook.

―

That evening, the Pathfinder was talking to Sergeant Dunham.

'Pathfinder, my old friend,' Dunham said. 'You must speak to Mabel about marriage. You must marry my daughter soon. That is my plan. You will be my son-in-law. You and Mabel will have children. I will be very happy.'

'But will Mabel be happy?' the Pathfinder asked. 'Does she want to marry me? I will be old soon and Mabel is very young – she is nineteen. Does Mabel want to marry me?'

'Mabel is a good girl,' Sergeant Dunham replied. 'I will tell her about my plan. She will do anything for me.'

The Pathfinder smiled. He liked the sergeant very much. Dunham had been his friend for many years. But was the sergeant's plan a good plan? The Pathfinder did not know.

'I will speak to Mabel soon,' the scout said.

The same evening, Lieutenant Muir – Mabel's third admirer – was talking to Major Lundie. Major Lundie was the commander of the 55th Regiment.

Lieutenant Muir was about fifty years old. He had been married three times, but all his wives had died.

'I am lonely,' Muir told the commander. 'I want to get married again, Major. I want to marry Sergeant Dunham's daughter.'

'You are fifty, Lieutenant Muir,' said Major Lundie. 'Mabel Dunham is nineteen. She will not marry you!'

'I am a lieutenant – an officer,' said Muir. 'Mabel is a sergeant's daughter. She will have a good life with me. She will be an officer's wife. Please tell Mabel's father about my plan. You are the commander of the regiment, sir. Sergeant Dunham will listen to you.'

'I do not like your plan, Lieutenant Muir,' said Major Lundie. 'But I will speak to the sergeant.'

The next day, Major Lundie spoke to Sergeant Dunham. The sergeant came to the major's house inside the fort. First, the two men talked about Dunham's journey to the Thousand Islands.

'Sergeant, you must stay at the Thousand Islands for one month,' Major Lundie said. 'After that, we will not use the blockhouse again. You must burn it! Jasper Western will come with the ship. He will bring you and your men back to Fort Oswego.'

'Now I have to ask you about a different thing,' said Major Lundie. 'Lieutenant Muir has spoken to me about your daughter. He wants to marry Mabel. What do you say, Sergeant? Do you say yes? And will Mabel say yes? Will she marry the Lieutenant?'

'Sir,' Dunham said. 'Mabel is going to marry the Pathfinder. She cannot marry Lieutenant Muir.'

'I did not like Lieutenant Muir's plan,' said Major Lundie. 'He is thirty years older than Mabel. But the Pathfinder is much older than Mabel too. Does she want to marry him?'

'She does not know about my plan, sir,' said Dunham. 'I have not told her about it. And the Pathfinder has not spoken to her. But Mabel will do anything for me, sir.'

Major Lundie was silent for a few moments. Then he spoke.

'I will tell Lieutenant Muir your answer, Sergeant,' said Major Lundie.

That evening, Major Lundie told Lieutenant Muir about Mabel and the Pathfinder. Lieutenant Muir was very angry.

'I will talk to Mabel,' he said. 'I am an officer. The Pathfinder is a scout! His friends are Indians! Mabel must not marry him! She must marry me!'

Muir was silent for a minute. Then he spoke again.

'Sir, I want to go to the Thousand Islands with Sergeant Dunham's men,' he said. 'Mabel is going to go with them. The Pathfinder is going to go with them. I want to go with them too!'

'No, Lieutenant Muir!' Major Lundie said. 'I will not send an officer to the Thousand Islands. Sergeant Dunham will be the commander of the men.'

'Sir, I want to be with Mabel,' said Muir. 'Please let me go to the Thousand Islands. I will not be a soldier there. I will be Mabel's friend. Dunham will be the commander at the blockhouse.'

Major Lundie was not happy about Lieutenant Muir's plan. The two men talked about it for a long time.

'I will let you go, Lieutenant,' Lundie said. 'But Sergeant Dunham will be the commander on the island.'

'Thank you, sir,' said Lieutenant Muir.

'You must leave the fort on Tuesday evening,' said Major Lundie. 'On Monday morning, there will be a shooting competition. There are many good marksmen at Fort Oswego, Lieutenant Muir. Who is the best marksman? There will be a prize for the best marksman. The prize will be a ladies' silk hat. The winner will give the hat to a lady!'

'I will win the competition, sir,' said Lieutenant Muir. 'And I will give the hat to Mabel Dunham!'

Lieutenant Muir left the room. Major Lundie smiled.

'Will he win the prize?' he asked himself.

There were three excellent marksmen at Fort Oswego.

'Yes! Those three men are better marksmen than all the soldiers,' Major Lundie said to himself. 'And those three marksmen will want to win the hat!'

The three best marksmen at Fort Oswego were Lieutenant Muir, Jasper Western, and the Pathfinder!

5

The Shooting Competition

On Monday morning, forty marksmen left the fort. They walked to some flat ground, near the shore of the lake. Major Lundie put a target on a wooden post. The target was two hundred feet from the marksmen. The men shot at the target, one after another.

Fifteen men hit the middle of the target with their bullets. Those marksmen were going to shoot again.

The major put a new target on the post. Then he moved the post. He put it three hundred feet from the marksmen.

The fifteen men shot at the target. Six men hit the middle of the target. Those marksmen were going to shoot again.

Major Lundie moved the post again. The new target was four hundred feet from the marksmen. The six men shot at it. This time, three men hit the middle of the target with their bullets. The three marksmen were Lieutenant Muir, Jasper Western and the Pathfinder!

Then Major Lundie took three potatoes from his pocket.

'I will throw these potatoes into the air,' he said to the three men. 'Each of you must shoot at a potato. Your bullet must hit the potato in the air.'

The Pathfinder smiled and he looked at Jasper. But Jasper was worried and unhappy.

'You will win the competition, Pathfinder,' Jasper said sadly. 'You are the best marksman in the regiment.'

The Pathfinder did not understand.

'Why is Jasper sad?' he asked himself. 'Jasper is a better sailor than I am. I am not worried about this. I am a better marksman than Jasper. Why is Jasper worried about that?'

'Do you want to win this competition, Jasper?' the scout asked his young friend.

'Yes, Pathfinder,' said the sailor. 'I want to win the competition very much. I will give the hat to Mabel!'

The Pathfinder smiled sadly. 'Mabel is going to be my wife,' he said to himself. 'I must tell Jasper about that soon.'

A moment later, Major Lundie shouted, 'Lieutenant Muir! You must shoot first.'

Major Lundie threw the first potato high into the air. Lieutenant Muir shot at it. The potato fell to the ground and the major picked it up. Muir's bullet had not hit the potato.

Jasper was going to shoot second. The major threw the second potato high into the air.

The potato fell to the ground. There was a hole in the middle of it.

Then Major Lundie threw the third potato into the air. The Pathfinder shot at it.

But the scout's bullet did not hit the potato.

Jasper had won the competition. Major Lundie gave the beautiful silk hat to Jasper. And Jasper gave the hat to Mabel. The young woman smiled happily.

―――

Later that day, Mabel was walking by the lake with the Pathfinder. The scout was carrying his gun and Mabel was wearing her new silk hat. The young woman looked at the scout. She liked her father's friend very much, but she did not understand him. He was sad. Why was he sad?

Suddenly, the Pathfinder looked up. Two hundred feet from them, two birds were flying across the sky. The Pathfinder lifted his gun and he waited.

For a second, one of the birds was between the scout's gun and the other bird. The Pathfinder fired his gun once, but both birds fell into the lake.

The Pathfinder had killed the two birds with one bullet! He smiled sadly.

'Goodbye, Mabel,' he said and he walked away.

He was telling the young woman something. He was not using words, he was using his gun. The Pathfinder was telling Mabel, 'I am a better marksman than Jasper. I did not *try* to win the competition.'

6

A Strange Letter

On Tuesday afternoon, Sergeant Dunham visited Major Lundie.

'Jasper Western has come to the fort with the ship,' Lundie said. 'The ship is waiting at the pier. You will leave in one hour. But first, I must tell you something. A strange letter has arrived. I am very worried.'

The major picked up a piece of paper and he gave it to Dunham. The sergeant read the words on the paper.

> Major Lundie
> Jasper Western is a traitor. He is working for the French Army. He tells the French soldiers about the 55th Regiment's plans. Your soldiers must watch him carefully. Then they must arrest him.
> A friend.

'I do not believe this letter, sir,' said Sergeant Dunham. 'Jasper Western is a good man. He is not a traitor. Who wrote this letter? He calls himself a friend. But he does not give his name!'

'I do not believe the letter,' said Major Lundie. 'But you must be very careful tomorrow. You will be the commander of those twelve soldiers. Their journey to the Thousand Islands is very important. It must be a safe journey!'

'You must watch Western carefully,' said Major Lundie. 'Does he send messages to the French? That is my question. And you must tell me the answer. What will the answer be? No? Then I will be happy! Yes? Then you must arrest him! Mr Cap will sail the ship. He will bring Western back to the fort.'

'I will be careful, sir,' said Sergeant Dunham. 'I will watch Jasper. But I do not believe this letter!'

Sergeant Dunham left Major Lundie and he talked to the Pathfinder. He told the scout about the strange letter.

'I do not believe the letter, Sergeant,' said the Pathfinder. 'Jasper is not a traitor. But there *is* a traitor at Fort Oswego. The French soldiers always know this regiment's plans. Who is the traitor? I do not know. But Jasper isn't the traitor!'

Sergeant Dunham and the twelve other soldiers were going to travel to the blockhouse on the ship. Lieutenant Muir, the Pathfinder, Charlie Cap, Mabel and another woman were going with the soldiers. The other woman was the wife of Corporal McNab – one of the soldiers.

At half past five, all these people went to the pier at the edge of the lake.

Chingachgook was not going to travel on the ship.

He was going to walk to the Thousand islands. He was going to look for French soldiers and their Mingo friends. Then he was going to meet Sergeant Dunham's soldiers at the blockhouse after four days.

The regiment's ship was waiting at the pier. It was a large wooden boat with three big sails. In the middle of the deck, there was one very large gun – a cannon.

Everybody got onto the ship. The soldiers and the women went down into the cabins. The cabins were rooms below the deck. Sergeant Dunham, Jasper and four other sailors stood on the deck.

At seven o'clock, the sailors pulled up the sails of the ship. Then the ship left the pier. Sergeant Dunham talked to Jasper.

'It will be dark soon,' Jasper said. 'We will travel all night. There are French boats on the lake, but they will not see us in the dark.'

7
On the Lake

It was early on Wednesday morning, the Pathfinder was talking to Jasper Western on the deck of the ship. Jasper was steering the ship and two of his sailors were on the deck. All the other travellers were asleep in the cabins, below the deck.

The ship was near the shore, and it was travelling towards the east end of the lake. It was travelling towards the great St Lawrence River.

The weather was fine, but Jasper was worried. He looked at the sky.

'We travelled a long way last night,' the young sailor said to the Pathfinder. 'That is good! I want to arrive at the Thousand Islands before this evening. But the weather is going to change. There will be bad weather this afternoon. There will be a storm!'

Jasper looked at the sky again. But the Pathfinder was not looking at the sky. He was looking at something on the lake.

'Look, Jasper!' he said. 'There is a canoe. There are two Indians in it. Are they watching us? Are they working for the French Army?'

Jasper called Cap, Dunham and the soldiers and sailors from the cabins. All the men ran up onto the deck of the ship. Jasper steered the ship towards the canoe. Soon the ship was very close to it.

Charlie Cap spoke to his brother-in-law.

'Arrowhead and Morning Dew are in the canoe,' he said. 'They are working for the French. Arrest them!'

'Stop!' Dunham shouted to the Tuscarora and his wife. 'You must come onto our ship. We are going to ask you some questions!'

Three of the soldiers pointed their guns at the Indians. Arrowhead looked at the guns. Then he stopped paddling the canoe.

Jasper's sailors pulled down the sails of the ship. Then they picked up the heavy anchor from the deck. The anchor was fixed to a long chain. The sailors threw the anchor into the water. In a moment, the ship stopped.

Arrowhead climbed onto the deck of the ship.

'Arrowhead, you are working for the French!' Sergeant Dunham said to the Tuscarora. 'I am going to arrest you! I am going to lock you in a cabin. Tomorrow, you must go back to Fort Oswego on this ship. Major Lundie will ask you some questions!'

'No! You are wrong!' Arrowhead said. 'We are not working for the French. We are working for the English, but our work is secret. You must let us go!'

Dunham talked to the Pathfinder and to Jasper Western. They did not believe Arrowhead's words.

'I will not let you go. You must go back to the fort,' Sergeant Dunham told the Indian. 'You must tell your story to Major Lundie.'

Arrowhead looked at the soldiers. He looked at their guns.

'I will go,' he said. 'But I must bring some things from my canoe. And I must bring my wife.'

'Go quickly!' said Dunham.

Arrowhead climbed down into his canoe. Quietly, he spoke to Morning Dew. Then suddenly, he picked up his paddle. He started to paddle the canoe very fast. He paddled towards the shore of the lake.

'Stop! Stop! We will shoot!' Dunham shouted.

Some of the soldiers lifted their guns and they shot at the Tuscaroras. But their bullets did not hit the Indians or the canoe. Soon, Arrowhead and Morning Dew were at the shore of the lake. They jumped out of the canoe and they ran into the forest.

'They have escaped!' said the Pathfinder angrily. 'They *are* working for the French. We will not catch them now. We must go on to the Thousand Islands.'

The sailors pulled the ship's anchor out of the water. They put it back on the deck. Then they pulled up the sails. Soon, the ship was sailing towards the east end of the lake again.

In one of the cabins below the deck, Sergeant Dunham was talking to Charlie Cap, the Pathfinder and Mabel.

'Our sails were down and our anchor was in the water,' Dunham said. 'We could not catch the Indians. Was that Jasper's plan? Is he a traitor? Is he working for the French?'

Charlie Cap did not like Jasper. And he wanted to be the captain of the ship.

'Yes! Jasper *is* a traitor!' he said. 'He is Arrowhead's friend. You must arrest him, Sergeant! Put him in a cabin and lock the door. I will take him back to Fort Oswego tomorrow.'

Mabel started to cry.

'You are wrong, Uncle!' she said. 'Jasper is a good man. He is not a traitor.'

'Yes! Mabel is right and you are wrong, Mr Cap!' said the Pathfinder. 'Jasper is not a traitor.'

But Sergeant Dunham was worried.

'My men are in danger,' he said. 'I must be careful. I will write a letter to Major Lundie. Charlie, you must take Jasper and my letter to the major tomorrow!'

Mabel and the Pathfinder were very sad. But they could not help Jasper.

The sergeant spoke to his brother-in-law again.

'Can you sail this ship to the Thousand Islands?' he asked. 'Jasper knows Lake Ontario well, but you have never sailed on this lake.'

'I have been a sailor all my life,' said Cap. 'I am a good sailor. I will sail the ship to the Thousand Islands! Where are the maps of the lake?'

'There are no maps,' said Dunham. 'Jasper knows every part of this lake. But he has never seen a map!'

Cap was worried. But he wanted to be the captain of the ship.

'I will sail this ship to the Thousand Islands!' he said again.

Ten minutes later, Sergeant Dunham had locked Jasper in a cabin.

———

Charlie Cap was standing on the deck of the ship and he was talking to the sailors.

'I am the captain of this ship now,' Cap said to the sailors.

The sailors were not happy. Lake Ontario was very dangerous and Cap had never sailed on it.

'There will be a storm soon,' one of the sailors said to Cap. 'You do not know the calm places on the lake. And there are no maps of the lake. How will you find the Thousand Islands?'

'Be quiet!' Cap shouted.

The ship travelled on towards the east. But an hour later, the storm started.

8
The Storm

The storm was terrible. The noise of thunder was very loud and the wind was very strong. The wind pushed the ship away from the shore. It pushed the ship towards the middle of the lake. Hour after hour, the rain fell. Charlie Cap was very worried.

'Jasper will help you,' the Pathfinder said to him.

'No, Pathfinder!' said Cap. 'Western is a traitor. I am the captain of this ship.'

'You are the captain!' said the Pathfinder angrily. 'But soon, you will be dead! Soon, we will all be dead!'

All that afternoon, and all that night, the wind pushed the ship away from the east end of the lake. It pushed the ship towards the west.

Daylight came. The Pathfinder and Sergeant Dunham were on the deck with Charlie Cap. The weather was very bad. The rain was falling very heavily. The noise of the wind was very loud. But there was another noise. It was a very deep noise. It was louder than the noise of the wind.

'Where are we, Charlie?' the sergeant asked his brother-in-law. 'And what is that terrible noise?'

'Where are we?' said Cap. 'I don't know!'

The Pathfinder looked around him. He looked at the shore of the lake. He listened to the terrible noise.

'The wind has pushed the ship towards the west end of the lake,' he said. 'The noise is the sound of the huge waterfall at Niagara!'

'I don't believe you,' said Cap angrily.

'But it is true,' said the Pathfinder.

Ten minutes later, the ship was near the south shore of the lake. Half a mile away, there were many sharp, dangerous rocks. The rocks were in the water, near the shore. And the wind was pushing the ship towards the rocks.

'The ship will hit those rocks,' the Pathfinder said to Dunham. 'And the ship will break into many pieces. You must bring Jasper up to the deck. Bring him now!'

'No!' shouted Cap. Quickly, he spoke to the sailors. They pulled down the ship's sails. Then they picked up the anchor and they threw it into the water. But the ship did not stop moving. The wind was pushing it towards the rocks. And the ship was pulling the anchor along the bottom of the lake.

Suddenly, Mabel came up onto the deck.

'Father!' she shouted. 'We are all going to die! I am afraid. Please bring Jasper. He will save us.'

Sergeant Dunham looked at his daughter. Then he ran down to the cabins below the deck. A minute later, he returned with Jasper.

'Charlie,' Dunham said to Cap. 'Jasper Western is the captain of this ship again. Listen to him!'

Jasper looked around him. He looked at the sky and he looked at the shore of the lake. Then he pointed to a place between two very large rocks.

'Steer the ship between those rocks!' he shouted to the sailors. 'There is a calm place behind them. The ship will be safe there. The storm will finish soon.'

'No!' shouted Cap. Then spoke to Dunham.

'Don't trust the young man!' Charlie said. 'He is a traitor! He wants to kill us!'

'Be quiet, Mr Cap,' said the Pathfinder. 'You have brought us to a terrible, dangerous place. Now Jasper will save us.'

The sailors pulled the ship's anchor onto the deck. They did not pull up the sails. One of them steered the ship carefully between the rocks. Behind the rocks, the water was calm. The sailors threw the anchor into the water again. After a few seconds, the ship stopped moving.

Two hours later, the storm finished. And Jasper started to sail the ship back towards the east end of Lake Ontario. On the afternoon of the next day, the ship arrived at the Thousand Islands at last.

The Thousand Islands was a strange place. There were many, many islands in the lake, near the shore. They were very near each other, and some of the islands were very small. Trees and bushes covered all the islands.

Jasper sailed the ship to one of the largest islands. The regiment's blockhouse was here. It was in a clearing in the middle of the island. Nobody could see the blockhouse from the lake. Jasper stopped the ship next to the shore of the island.

Sergeant Dunham and his men quickly left the ship. Soon, the other travellers were standing on the shore with them. The sailors stayed on the deck of the ship.

Sergeant Dunham spoke to one of his soldiers.

'Go to the blockhouse, Corporal McNab,' he said. 'Bring the other soldiers here. They must leave immediately.'

The corporal ran through the trees. A few minutes

later, he returned with twelve other soldiers. The twelve men climbed onto the ship.

Then Sergeant Dunham spoke to his brother-in-law.

'Jasper is not a traitor,' the sergeant said. 'Jasper will take the ship back to Fort Oswego. You will stay here with us.'

———

Sergeant Dunham and his soldiers walked through the trees, towards the middle of the island. Mabel, Mrs McNab, the Pathfinder, Lieutenant Muir and Charlie Cap walked behind them.

Soon, they came to the clearing and they saw the blockhouse. It was a strong wooden building with two storeys.

'We will rest now,' Sergeant Dunham said. 'Tomorrow, we will start our work. We will watch the French ships!'

9

Morning Dew

The next morning, Sergeant Dunham told Mabel about his plans.

'I am going to another island with nine soldiers,' he said. 'There are four canoes here. We will go to the island in two of the canoes. That island is further north than this one. Today and tomorrow, we will watch the French ships. We will return here tomorrow evening.'

'The Pathfinder will go to the eastern shore of the lake,' said Sergeant Dunham. 'He will try to meet Chingachgook. But he will return tomorrow evening too. Corporal McNab and two other soldiers will stay here with you, your Uncle Charlie, Mrs McNab, and Lieutenant Muir.'

'I don't like Lieutenant Muir,' said Mabel.

'The Lieutenant wants to marry you,' said Dunham. 'He told Major Lundie about it. He wants to be near you. But you don't like him and I don't like him, Mabel.'

Soon, Sergeant Dunham and his nine soldiers found the canoes. The soldiers got into two of the canoes. Quickly, they paddled away from the island. They paddled towards the north. Then the Pathfinder got into another canoe and he paddled towards the east.

An hour later, Mabel was walking through the trees on the island. Suddenly she heard a noise in front of her. Then she saw Lieutenant Muir.

Lieutenant Muir was tying a piece of red cloth to a tree near the shore.

'Why is he doing that?' Mabel asked herself. 'Is he sending a message to someone?'

Muir did not see Mabel. He got into the last canoe. Very quietly, he paddled away from the island.

Mabel was worried. Something was wrong! A moment later, she heard another noise. Somebody was calling her name!

Mabel looked across the water. About two hundred feet from the shore, to the east, there was another island. Mabel saw somebody coming from the trees on that island. It was an Indian woman and she was pulling a small canoe. The woman was Morning Dew!

Morning Dew pushed her canoe into the water. She got into the canoe and she paddled across the water, to Mabel.

'Miss Mabel,' the Indian woman said. 'This is a very dangerous place. Your enemies are near. You must go into the blockhouse with the other woman. You must put something across the door.'

'Arrowhead is here with many Mingos,' Morning Dew said. 'They know about the blockhouse. The French soldiers know about it too. And they know your father's plans. The Mingos are going to attack this island today! They will kill the three soldiers. Then they will wait. Tomorrow the other soldiers will return. The Mingos will kill them too!'

'Why are you telling me this, Morning Dew?' Mabel asked. 'This is Arrowhead's plan, and you love Arrowhead.'

'Yes, I love Arrowhead,' said Morning Dew. 'But I love you too. You were kind to me, Miss Mabel. You must hide now. Arrowhead will come. He must not see you. He will kill your friends and he will take you away!'

'He will take me away?' said Mabel. 'Will he kill me?'

'No!' said Morning Dew. 'Arrowhead will not kill you. He wants a new wife. He wants you!'

'But *you* are his wife, Morning Dew,' said Mabel.

'Indian men have many wives,' said Morning Dew angrily. 'I must go now. Arrowhead will see me here. He will see me talking to you. He will kill me!'

Morning Dew paddled back across the water, to the other island. She pulled her canoe out of the water. Then she ran towards the trees.

Mabel went to the blockhouse. She told Morning Dew's news to Corporal McNab and his wife. But she could not find Charlie Cap.

'Go into the blockhouse with my wife,' said Corporal McNab. 'I'll wait for the Mingos.' He picked up his gun.

Ten minutes later, Mabel and Mrs McNab were sitting in the blockhouse. They were looking out of a window in the upper storey. They had put a heavy piece of wood across the door of the blockhouse. Nobody could get into the building.

Suddenly, they heard shouts, screams and the sound of guns. And they saw many Indians running from the trees. Corporal McNab ran to the blockhouse.

'The Mingos have killed the two other soldiers,' he shouted to the women. 'Stay there. I will bring help!'

McNab ran towards the shore. But three Indians saw him. They ran towards him. McNab shot one of the Indians but the other two jumped on him. They killed him with knives.

Mrs McNab saw the Indians kill her husband. She screamed. Then she ran downstairs and out of the door.

A moment later, Mrs McNab was dead. Suddenly, Mabel heard a noise below her. Somebody had come into the blockhouse! Mabel heard somebody putting the piece of wood across the door. Was one of the Mingos going to kill her? She heard footsteps on the stairs. Then she heard a voice.

'I have closed the door, Miss Mabel,' said Morning Dew. 'You are safe!'

10
In the Blockhouse

The afternoon passed. Outside the blockhouse, the Mingos were sitting and waiting. Fifteen of the Indians sat on the ground and they watched the blockhouse.

At four o'clock, four more Indians came to the blockhouse. One of them was Arrowhead. The Indians brought Lieutenant Muir and Charlie Cap with them. The two white men were tied with ropes.

Arrowhead shouted up to Mabel.

'Open the door, Miss Mabel!' he shouted. 'Open the door. I will let you return to Fort Oswego. And I will let these men go with you.'

'Do not believe him, Miss Mabel,' Morning Dew said quietly. 'You must not trust him. He will not let you go.'

Mabel shouted to the Tuscarora.

'I do not trust you, Arrowhead!'

Then Lieutenant Muir shouted up to the young woman.

'The Indians are going to kill us, Mabel. Please open the door. Arrowhead will not hurt you.'

But Charlie Cap shouted too.

'Do not open the door, Mabel! Do not trust these men!'

'Be quiet!' Arrowhead said angrily. 'I will kill you!'

'I am old. But I am not afraid to die,' said Cap.

The Indians did not kill Cap and Muir. But they took the two white men away.

'What are the Indians going to do now?' Mabel asked Morning Dew.

'Arrowhead is waiting for a French army officer,' the Tuscarora woman said. 'The Frenchman is Arrowhead's commander.'

Mabel was worried and unhappy. But suddenly she saw another Indian. He was standing in the trees, at the edge of the clearing. It was the Mohican, Chingachgook!

Chingachgook watched the Mingos for a few minutes. Then he looked at the blockhouse and he lifted his hand. Quickly and quietly, he walked away.

'Chingachgook was sending me a message,' Mabel said to herself. 'He will bring help.'

———

The next morning, Mabel looked out of the window. The Mingos were outside the blockhouse. They had made a small fire. They were eating some food.

At midday, a soldier came and sat with the Indians. He was a French officer. Arrowhead was with him. The two men talked for an hour. Then the Frenchman went away.

At three o'clock, Arrowhead stood up. He spoke to the other Indians. Then he walked away from the clearing. Some of the Mingos followed him.

'Arrowhead is waiting for the other English soldiers,' said Morning Dew. 'They will return soon. Then the Mingos will kill them.' The Tuscarora woman laughed.

'I must tell my father about Arrowhead's plan,' Mabel said. 'I must help my father and his friends.'

'You cannot help them,' said Morning Dew. 'I will not let you leave. You must stay here!'

———

At seven o'clock, it was dark again. Mabel heard somebody knocking on the door. She went downstairs.

'Who is there?' she said quietly.

'The Pathfinder,' said a voice on the other side of the door. 'Please open the door, Miss Mabel!'

Mabel quickly opened the door, and the scout came into the blockhouse.

'Don't be afraid, Miss Mabel,' the Pathfinder said. 'I met Chingachgook yesterday evening. He will find Jasper. Jasper will bring the ship back to the Thousand Islands. He will bring some soldiers.'

'I am worried about my father,' said Mabel. 'The Mingos are waiting for him and his men.'

At that moment, they heard the sound of guns.

'The Indians are attacking Father and his soldiers!' Mabel shouted. 'We must help them.'

'We cannot help them now,' said the Pathfinder.

Ten minutes later, they heard noises outside the door. And they heard the voice of Charlie Cap.

The Pathfinder opened the door carefully. Charlie Cap and Sergeant Dunham came into the blockhouse. Cap was holding his brother-in-law. There was a lot of blood on the sergeant's clothes.

'The other soldiers are dead,' said Cap. 'Your father is badly injured, Mabel. You must take care of him.'

'Is Lieutenant Muir dead?' the Pathfinder asked.

'I have not seen Lieutenant Muir,' said Cap. 'I escaped from the Indians and I found the English soldiers. The Indians attacked us, but we fought them. Lieutenant Muir was not with the Mingos. But he was not with our soldiers.'

The Pathfinder put the heavy piece of wood across the door.

'We are safe until the morning,' he said.

Sergeant Dunham was very badly injured. Soon, he was asleep.

In the morning, Sergeant Dunham opened his eyes.

Mabel, I am dying. Please make a promise. Please marry my friend, the Pathfinder.

Yes, Father. I will marry the Pathfinder.

A few minutes later, Sergeant Dunham died.

Father is dead.

I will take care of you now, Mabel.

Suddenly, Mabel and the Pathfinder heard the voice of Arrowhead.

'Come out of the blockhouse now!' he shouted. 'We are going to burn it!'

Mabel looked out of the window. She saw some of the Mingos carrying pieces of wood. They put the wood against the wall of the blockhouse. Arrowhead was standing by the small fire. He was holding a branch from a tree. The Tuscarora put one end of it into the fire for a few seconds. Then he walked towards the blockhouse with the burning branch.

But at that moment, there was a very loud noise.

'That was the sound of the ship's cannon!' said the Pathfinder. 'Jasper has arrived!'

Mabel and the scout heard the sound of the cannon again and again.

Then Jasper, Chingachgook and twelve English soldiers were running towards the blockhouse. And soon they had killed most of the Mingos. The other Indians ran away.

The Pathfinder met Jasper outside the blockhouse.

'You came quickly, my friend,' said the Pathfinder.

'I was worried about all of you,' Jasper replied. 'I am not a traitor. But there *is* a traitor here. And there was great danger for you here. I knew that. I did not go to Fort Oswego. I turned the ship and I came back. Chingachgook met us near the shore. He told us about the Mingos.'

A few minutes later, the soldiers found Arrowhead

and the French officer. The two men were getting into a canoe. They were trying to escape from the island. The English soldiers took them to the blockhouse.

Then suddenly, Lieutenant Muir walked out of the trees. Muir went to the blockhouse with the others. Outside the building, he spoke to the Pathfinder.

'I escaped from the Indians,' he said quietly. 'I killed two of them!'

The scout did not reply. He took the Frenchman's gun. He took Arrowhead's gun too.

'We will not kill you,' he said to them. 'We will take your guns but we will let you go.'

'We must leave this island soon, Jasper,' the Pathfinder said. 'The French Army has known about this blockhouse for a long time. We will burn the building tomorrow. Then we will go back to Fort Oswego.'

The French officer smiled. 'Yes,' he said. 'You must go. There is a traitor in your regiment. We know all your plans.' He laughed.

'Western is the traitor,' Lieutenant Muir said. 'I am going to arrest him!'

The Pathfinder was surprised. The French officer was surprised. And Arrowhead was surprised too!

'No!' the Tuscarora said. 'You are —'

Suddenly, Lieutenant Muir took a knife from his pocket and he attacked the Tuscarora. But Arrowhead had a knife too. He pushed it into Muir's body. The English soldier fell to the ground. He was dead.

Arrowhead started to run towards the trees. But Chingachgook ran after him. The Mohican quickly caught Arrowhead. The two men fought.

Chingachgook was old but he was strong. He took Arrowhead's knife from the Tuscarora's hand. A moment later, Arrowhead was dead!

The French officer looked at the body of Lieutenant Muir.

'This man was the traitor,' he said to the Pathfinder. 'The French Army paid him money. He told us your secrets. He wrote a letter to your commander – a letter about the captain of your ship. The Lieutenant worked for us, but he was a bad man. He was a traitor to his country. Good soldiers are not traitors!'

Then the French officer turned and he walked away.

11
'Do You Love Me?'

The next day, the Pathfinder, Chingachgook and Jasper buried Arrowhead and the dead soldiers. Then they burnt the blockhouse. After that, they were going to take Mabel and Cap back to the fort.

But first, the Pathfinder spoke to Mabel and Jasper.

'Mabel,' he said. 'I love you. I want to marry you. Your father wanted that too. Will you marry me, dear Mabel?'

'I loved my father very much,' said Mabel. 'He told me about his plan yesterday. He was dying. I told him, "I will marry the Pathfinder." I made a promise to him. Pathfinder, I will marry you.'

The Pathfinder was happy. He smiled. But then he looked carefully at Mabel. And he looked at Jasper. Mabel was sad. And Jasper was sad too.

'Do you love *me*, Mabel?' the scout asked quietly.

For a moment, Mabel did not answer.

Then she said, 'No, Pathfinder. I like you very much, but I don't love you.'

'Do you love Jasper?' the Pathfinder asked.

Mabel started to cry. 'Yes,' she said. 'I love Jasper.'

'Jasper, do you love Mabel?' the Pathfinder asked the young sailor.

'Yes, I love her,' the young man answered sadly.

The Pathfinder thought for a few moments. Then

he spoke quickly.

'Mabel, you must be happy!' he said. 'Forget about your promise to your father. He is dead. You do not love me. You must not marry me! Go back to Fort Oswego with Jasper. Marry him. I will stay here. I will take care of Morning Dew. I will take her back to her people. Then Chingachgook and I will travel to the Hudson River. You will not meet me again.'

'You are a good man, Pathfinder,' said Jasper.

'Yes, you are a good man, Pathfinder,' said Mabel. She kissed him quickly. Then she held Jasper's hand and the two young people walked towards the ship.

Published by Macmillan Heinemann ELT
Between Towns Road, Oxford OX4 3PP
Macmillan Heinemann ELT is an imprint of
Macmillan Publishers Limited
Companies and representatives throughout the world
Heinemann is a registered trademark of Harcourt Education, used under licence.

ISBN 1-405072-31-8
EAN 978-1-405072-31-1

This retold version by T. P. Yatt for Macmillan Readers
First published 1998
Text © T. P. Yatt 1998, 2005
Design and illustration © Macmillan Publishers Limited 1998, 2005

This edition first published 2005

All rights reserved; no part of this publication may be reproduced,
stored in a retrieval system, transmitted in any form, or by any means,
electronic, mechanical, photocopying, recording, or otherwise, without
the prior written permission of the publishers.

Illustrated by Annabel Large
Map on page 3 and illustrations on page 5 by John Gilkes
Typography by Adrian Hodgkins
Designed by Sue Vaudin
Original cover template design by Jackie Hill
Cover photography by Corbis
Acknowledgements: The publishers would like to thank Popperfoto for
permission to reproduce the picture on page 4.

Printed in Thailand

2009 2008 2007 2006 2005
10 9 8 7 6 5 4 3 2